Poems & Prayers

Robin Swenor Shattuck

WestBow
PRESS
A DIVISION OF THOMAS NELSON

WestBow Press books may be ordered through booksellers or by contacting:

WestBow Press
A Division of Thomas Nelson
1663 Liberty Drive
Bloomington, IN 47403
www.westbowpress.com
1-(866) 928-1240

Because of the dynamic nature of the Internet, any web addresses or links contained in this book may have changed since publication and may no longer be valid. The views expressed in this work are solely those of the author and do not necessarily reflect the views of the publisher, and the publisher hereby disclaims any responsibility for them.

Any people depicted in stock imagery provided by Thinkstock are models, and such images are being used for illustrative purposes only.
Certain stock imagery © Thinkstock.

ISBN 978-1-4497-1673-8 (sc)
ISBN: 978-1-4497-1674-5 (e)
Library of Congress Control Number: 2011928728

Printed in the United States of America

WestBow Press rev. date: 5/19/2011

A word from the author:

I have written these poems over the past 30 years. They have been inspired by my times of sitting before the Lord in quiet stillness and listening to His voice. They come from my heart. In sharing them with you, I pray that you are inspired, refreshed, and encouraged.

Sincerely,
Robin Swenor Shattuck

This book is dedicated to Julie Flynn, my Petoskey High School Creative Writing instructor, the one who encouraged me to write what I feel and truly inspired me with her enthusiasm for teaching.

Thank you, Mrs. Flynn

Hope

The Child In Me

I am but a child,
young,
and still weak at times.
I am growing,
learning new things all the time…
and God isn't finished with me yet;
if He were, I would be perfect.
Still
He hasn't given up on me.
He is my teacher;
and He is so patient with me.
He helps me to learn from my mistakes
and helps me overcome my trials.
He gives me new strength.

Are you watching me grow?
Do you see how much I learn?
Will you help me in my weakness
and be a source of strength for me?
Will you be patient with me?
God hasn't given up on me,
so please…
don't you give up on me either.
I want you to be there for me.

We urge you, brethren, admonish the unruly, encourage the fainthearted, help the weak, be patient with everyone.

I Thessalonians 5:14
(New American Standard Bible)

Patient means to endure, to wait, or to put up with. And we should do this without complaining. According to this verse patience is not an option for Christians. Some are more patient than others. Is it easier to be patient with an adult or with a child? We need to teach those who don't know how to behave, those who don't have good manners. We need to be strong for those who are weak and those who are weary from stress in life. It's part of being a family.

Father,
Is there someone who needs me? Show me today who I can help. Show me today someone to whom I can offer my ear or my shoulder to cry on. And when I see someone who doesn't behave properly, help me to not pass judgment, but, rather, to reach out to that person and to teach that person what is right. Help me to love. Amen.

A Heavenly Breeze

A cool breeze blows through my being

cleansing my spirit

and making me whole.

It filters through every cell in my body

creating me anew.

This wind of life,

the breath of God,

my only hope for tomorrow.

Awake, O north wind, and come, thou south, blow upon my garden, that the spices therof may flow out. Let my beloved come into His garden, and eat His pleasant fruits.

Song of Solomon 4:16
(King James Version)

The wind of Life, the Breath of God, this is our hope for a life that is fruitful, a life that will produce much for God. Oh, we can strive on our own, but it's much easier to produce fruit in this life when God is in control. And when you take the time to lie down next to the quiet streams and be refreshed in God's presence it is much easier to feel the Wind of God blow on your garden.

Father,
Sometimes I get too busy to take time to relax in Your presence. Help me to slow down, relax, and be refreshed in You. I know that only then will I feel Your wind blow on my garden, and only then will the good fruit be produced in my life. Amen.

Who Am I?

Who am I?
Just another person roaming,
trying to find my way in this world?

What am I?
A young woman,
living, working, struggling from day to day?

Why am I here?
Is there a reason?
Do I belong?

Yes! I belong!
God put me here…
I am to bring others to Him!

I am a young woman
chosen by God
among millions of people…

I am God's child
living for Him each day…
a life of victory
which He has already planned out for me.

Before I formed you in the womb I knew you…

Jeremiah 1:5a
(New American Standard Bible)

We all have dreams and goals. Some are put there by God; some are conjured up in our own minds. It is our destiny to determine which ones are of God. It must be our desire to submit to His will and accomplish that which God put in us to do no matter how difficult it is, keeping in mind that if it is of God, He will give us the strength and means to accomplish what He calls us to do. Our greatest goal and desire should be to bring others to Christ.

Father,
Help me to know whatYou want me to do with my life. Give me the strength and finances to accomplish what You want me to do every day of my life. But, Father, most of all, help me to be sensitive to the needs of those around me. Help me to shine Your light in this dark world so that others may find You. Amen.

Just As He Promised

Just as flakes of snow gracefully and delicately fall
from their heavenly home for another season of winter…
Jesus willfully came down to earth,
a tiny babe,
born of a virgin, wrapped in soft clothes,
lying in His manger bed…

and just as the snow quickly unhesitantly melts away
for another season of spring…
Jesus courageously and doubtlessly left this earth,
an innocent man,
perfect and sinless,
bleeding, hurting,
hanging on a cross…

Just as another winter season will always come
bringing flurries of beautiful white, fluffy snow,
spring will also come
bringing with it the sun
to melt away the snow
and warm all the earth…

…so Jesus will also return to take those who know Him
back to His home to be with Him forever
just as He promised…

just as He promised…

For behold, the winter is past, the rain is over and gone…

Song of Solomon 2:11
(New American Standard Bible)

So let us know, let us press on to know the Lord, His going forth is as certain as the dawn, and He will come to us like the rain, like the spring rain watering the earth…

Hosea 6:3
(New American Standard Bible)

Something in us dies when the autumn leaves have fallen off the trees. Everything looks dead, dry, and barren. The trees in their nakedness wait for the cold harsh winter. Then it snows, and it is so beautiful again. And then we come alive again in spring when it begins to warm up again. The trees begin to bud, and the flowers begin to bloom. It's the rain that we long for. It's the rain that gives us life. It's knowing the depths of God's love and presence that sustains us.

Father,
Bring the rain again! I want to know You more, God! I want to feel Your presence. I want to know Your love. I want to feel Your passion, God. Please bring me rain again. Amen.

DEATH

cold, still

burying, crying, hurting

darkness, pain – freedom, light

unyielding, satisfying, glorifying

victorious, abundant

LIFE

Truly, I say to you, he who hears my word, and believes Him who sent me, has eternal life, and does not come into judgment, but has passed out of death into life.

John 5:24
(New American Standard Bible)

When someone you love dies, the pain can be so great, and the grief can be so deep, you think that you will never see light again. You may feel like this heavy weight will never be lifted. But if you know that your loved one knew Jesus, then you can have the promise that your loved one is waiting for you in heaven. You have hope that you will see your loved one again. Hold on to that hope.

Father,
Life…I want that abundant life here on this earth. And it only comes from knowing You. I want to know You, God. I want to pass from death into life knowing the God who created me. Amen.

Hope is...

A rainbow

Struggling up a mountain after being in the deep, dark valley

A ray of sunshine through storm clouds

Seeing the first robin after a cold, hard winter

Letting your light shine in the darkest night

Trusting that the Lord Jesus Christ will come again
to take His bride home

And you will have confidence, because there is hope.

Job 11:18a
(Revised Standard Version)

Be strong, and let your heart take courage, all you who hope in the Lord.

Psalm 31:24
(New American Standard Bible)

Through Him we have obtained access to this grace in which we stand, and we rejoice in our hope of sharing the glory of God.

Romans 5:2
(Revised Standard Version)

Big things can discourage us, but small things can give us hope.

You've had a long, hard day, and things were rough at the office. You're in a check-out line at the store with that necessary milk. The clerk smiles at you and very kindly says, "Have a nice evening." You can tell she sincerely means it – and she doesn't even know you. You suddenly have hope that this could actually be a nice evening. You were given a little bit of hope. Yes, little things matter.

Now, you go and be the one to give someone a little bit of hope today.

Father,
Help me to get beyond myself to see the needs of others. I want to touch someone's life today. I want to give someone hope. I want to show someone Christ. Show me who needs You. Amen.

Healing

I cried today:
I was hurting.
"Abba?", I called.

And that was all I had to say.
My Daddy picked me up
and put me on His lap.
He brushed my hair from my face
and wiped my tears.
He smiled at me
and made me laugh,
and then He held me close.

Abba didn't even have to say, "I love you."
And my hurt was gone.

Blessed be the God and Father of our Lord Jesus Christ, the Father of mercies and God of all comfort, who comforts us in all our affliction, so that we may be able to comfort those who are in any affliction, with the comfort with which we ourselves are comforted by God.

II Corinthians 1:3
(Revised Standard Version)

Imagine, the God of the universe loves you personally enough to comfort you, to wrap His big arms around you, to hold you, to make you feel better. The words of this verse give peace that God cares about us in a personal way. The word "Abba" means daddy. God, although He is the creator of all things, wants to be like a daddy to us. He wants to have that kind of personal relationship with us. He wants us to be able to climb upon His lap and snuggle with Him to be comforted, just as a child does with his daddy.

Abba, Father, Daddy,
I need You to comfort me when I'm sad or lonely or hurt or discouraged. You are the One who made me, and You can be the One to hold me and make me feel better. I know that You love me and You care about me. You care about the circumstances and trials I face. You want to be right in the middle of it all with me. Help me to turn to You first for the comfort that I need. Amen.

Give Them To Me

Give them to me,
said Jesus, my King.
Just leave them at the cross.

I want the things that burden you,
your problems and your loss.

You may think you can handle it,
but it always comes back to me.

I want to help you – I will never forsake you.
Oh, my child, can't you see?

I love you!
I gave up all I had in heaven
to come…to die for you.

Others hear my voice, and I know that you do,
so won't you trust in me, too?

So give them to me,
just leave them at my feet.
I will be the one true friend
you can count on to the end.

Cast your burden upon the Lord, and He will sustain you; He shall never suffer the righteous to be moved.
Psalm 55:22
(King James Version)

Giving your burdens to God releases you from a heaviness that shouldn't be yours to begin with. God never intended for His children to carry heavy loads. It is difficult to be joyful when you are burdened. Maybe today you need to consider what is weighing you down and give those burdens to the Lord; let Him carry the load. Or perhaps you need to call a good friend and share your burdens to make your load lighter. God gives us friends to help us carry our burdens.

Father,
I know You don't want me to carry this heavy burden. It gets so heavy sometimes that it's all I think about. Perhaps if I lay it down at Your feet, it will be easier to look up at You and see Your lovely face. Maybe it will also be easier for me to look around and see the needs of others. Yes, Lord, I give this burden to You so that I can be free. Amen.

Lord!
You were just putting the pieces
of the puzzle of my life all together
to form a beautiful picture –
one filled with
> the light of Your Son,
> the peace that passes all understanding,
> the joy that fills me to overflowing,
> because of the gift of Your Holy Spirit…

and then…
I took those pieces and slowly removed each one
and threw them in the box.
Now, Lord,
the lid is closing –
my joy and peace and light
are all diminishing…

Jesus,
open the lid again,
please…
I don't ever want control of my life again;
I want to be free in You.
Remake me, Lord;
lay the pieces back on the table,
and put me back together.
I'm Yours.

For You formed my inward parts, You wove me in my mother's womb. I will give thanks to You, for I am fearfully and wonderfully made, wonderful are Your works, and my soul knows it very well.

Psalm 139:13-14
(New American Standard Bible)

Why is it so easy for us to hold onto our worries and fears? Is it a comfort zone? Are we afraid to trust in God? Do we think that He won't take care of our problems? Or that He'll take care of the problem in a way that is different from what we want? Is it a control issue? We want to be in control?

Imagine that! God is God, the Creator of the universe. He knows when a star falls from the very place He put it. He moves mountains. He feeds the tiny sparrows. He knows how many hairs are on your head. He created you for a purpose, and He has a plan for your life. Trust Him to lead you.

Father,
You made me for a purpose. I want to discover Your plan for my life. I want to follow You. I don't want to put this puzzle together myself. I want You to do it for me. Remake me, Father. Make my life beautiful. Amen.

Meekly Mended

I had put my fragile being upon the top shelf where I wanted to be:
      recognized…
      significant…
      alone…
It didn't matter what anyone thought or said.
I know where I was,
but I didn't know the ground was not stable.
it shook…
and I alone had the farthest to fall.

Now here I am,
broken, hurt, but humbles.

And here You are to fix, to heal, and to lift me up,
because only You can still love me and live with me just the way I am.
You believe in me.
You trust me.
You care for me.

You are in me,
and I am in You,
and we are not alone.

Pride goes before destruction and haughtiness before a fall.
Proverbs 16:18
(New Living Translation)

He sat down, called the twelve disciples over to Him, and said, "Whoever wants to be first must take last place and be the servant of everyone else."
Mark 9:35
(New Living Translation)

The Bible is clear on what happens when we have too much pride. We fall. Humility makes you a great person. Jesus was the greatest person to ever live, and He was the greatest servant to ever live. Shouldn't we strive to serve more?

Father,
I want Your Holy Spirit to show me when I am prideful so that I can allow You to humble me before I fall. Help me to see the needs of those around me, and give me the desire to serve people more. I want to be more like Jesus. Amen.

Just A Touch

I was struggling to get through the crowd
to have You touch me, Lord.
But, Jesus, I was blinded by all my cares, and I couldn't see.
Yet I knew You were here –
everyone was following You and calling out Your name.

I dropped everything I had
and pushed my way through the crowd
until I saw You.
I had to have freedom;
the freedom that clothed You.
So I reached out and touched Your robe,
and the burden that I had carried to You was gone;
joy was in its place.

And then You said, "Who touched me?"

I fell at Your feet, oblivious to the crowd.
"I did, my Lord."

You told me, "Daughter, your faith has made you whole;
go in peace."

And I walked away –
someone new.

And behold, a woman who had suffered from a flow of blood for twelve years came up behind him and touched the fringe of his garment, for she kept saying to herself, "If I only touch His garment, I shall be restored to health."

Matthew 9:20-21
(Amplified Bible)

This woman may have felt she wasn't worthy of Jesus' attention, that she was insignificant. Her faith told her that all she had to do was touch His clothes, and she would be healed. She didn't just believe that it COULD happen; she believed that it WOULD happen. She had no doubt. Total trust leaves absolutely no room for doubt. How do you think she felt after she touched Jesus' clothes? She knew she was healed because she believed that she would be.

Jesus turned around and, seeing her, He said, "Take courage, daughter! Your faith has made you well." And at once the woman was restored to health.

Matthew 9:22
(Amplified Bible)

She probably didn't expect Jesus to even acknowledge her. But she already knew what His words would be. I like to think that she just sat on the ground in wonder at how good she must have felt knowing that the bleeding had stopped. She must have been suddenly full of energy and strength.

How much faith do you have?

Father,
All I need is faith the size of a mustard seed. I trust You, Father. I trust You with my whole heart. I know You have my best desire in mind. Amen.

Feelings

Words…
      they bruise,
      they cut,
      they kill,
Words, spoken in bitterness and anger attacked me
in a way I had never known before.

I bled.
and I died.

Words…
      they wash,
      they heal,
      they give life.
Words of apology, offered in meekness and humbleness,
cleansed me like raindrops in a desert.

      I melted.
      I forgave,
      and I live.

A gentle answer turns away wrath, but a harsh word stirs up anger.

Proverbs 15:1
(New American Standard Bible)

Words are powerful, whether they are positive or negative. The old saying, "Sticks and stones may break my bones, but words can never hurt me" just isn't true. Negative words can bruise or even break a person's spirit, and when the spirit is broken, it's harder for that person to heal. Positive words, on the other hand, encourage people and lift up their spirits. It is important to think before we speak, and it's important to choose our words carefully.

Father,
Help me to choose my words more carefully. Help me to think before I speak. Help me to speak positive words of affirmation into the lives of others so that they can be encouraged. And when I must correct those that I love, help to do so in love. Amen.

Fear or Love

Fear…
> An omnipotent sensation
> > It struggles –
> > strives…
> > It controls –
> > rules…
> Fear eliminates all freedom
> making you its slave.
> Fear drags you down
> plowing you under.

Fear…

> Like a lighted match
> burns and spreads
> Unless something greater
> puts it out.

Love…
> An omnipotent emotion
> > It overtakes –
> > overpowers…
> > It conquers –
> > triumphs…
> Love extinguishes all doubt
> making you believe.
> Love lifts you up
> making you glad.

Love…

> Like a river
> washes over you
> smoothing the roughness
> and making the road easier.

For God hath not given us a spirit of fear, but of power, and of love, and of a sound mind.

II Timothy 1:7
(King James Version)

Fear is the opposite of love. There can be no fear in pure love. God is love, and Satan is fear. So when we are afraid, we must run to God. As we get closer to Him we find the fear fading away. Fear cannot be where God is. The Word of God dispels darkness. So when we are afraid we can read the Word of God aloud, and fear will disappear.

Father,
Help me to recognize fear as being from the enemy. And help me to run to You as soon as I feel that emotion, knowing that when I run to You, the fear must leave. God, I want to know Your pure love. Your love is kind and gentle. I want to experience Your love, God, because in Your love is power and a sound mind. Draw me close, Father, I want to know Your love. Amen.

Dear Lord,

I am a lonely sheep,
But...
This is a different kind of loneliness.
I've been lonely when I was in a pasture full of friendly sheep.
I've been lonely simply because I withdrew from other sheep
      wanting some time.
But I've never been the new one in the flock,
standing in the lush green field with the freshest water flowing nearby,
      and yet no sheep reach out to me.
And you tell me, my Lord, that I need nothing except You...
      my Shepherd, my Constant Companion, my Contentment.

…being mindful of the words of the Lord Jesus, how He said, "It is more blessed to give than to receive."

Acts 20:35
(Amplified Bible)

What do we do when we are lonely?

We have two options:
1. Withdraw and be alone
2. Reach out to somebody and be a friend to someone else in need

If we withdraw, all we can see is ourselves. That sounds selfish. But when we reach out to somebody else, or pray for somebody else, we actually forget ourselves. When we get outside of our own little box, we become selfless. What does Jesus want? He wants us to be servants, because in serving, we don't think of ourselves, we think of others. When we serve, we give.

Father,
Help me to get outside of my own little world to see the needs of those around me. Help me to serve more and receive less. I want to be a servant like Jesus was. I want to give of myself. I don't want to be selfish. I want to be a friend to someone who needs a friend. Show me someone today who needs a friend. Show me someone who is lonely. Help me to show that person who Jesus is. Amen.

Abandoned Trust

I'm not comfortable in my present,
and my future is uncertain.
Is there somewhere I can go?
I need something I can trust in.

There must be someone out there
who can show me the right way.
There are many different paths to take,
and I don't want to go astray.

I'm sure there's only one right path;
there's only one way to go.
If I make the right decisions,
then the things in my life will flow.

It must be God who is in control.
He is the Creator of it all.
If I surrender my life to Him
then He'll catch me when I fall.

I have faith that He knows better
when I think that I know best.
Only He can see the future,
and in this I can rest.

So I will surrender
to the maker of my life,
and I will obey Him
to avoid all kinds of strife.

It was for freedom that Christ set us free; therefore, keep standing firm and do not be subject again to a yoke of slavery.

Galatians 5:1
(New American Standard Bible)

Surrender…what does that word mean? It seems that when we surrender, we are put in chains. For example, when a police officer wants to arrest someone, that person surrenders, and handcuffs are put on him. He is then in bondage. However, in the spirit realm, the opposite is true. Apart from God, we are in bondage to sin. But when we surrender to God, the chains fall off, and we are free! It sounds like a paradox: surrender to God is freedom to our soul.

Father,
I surrender all to You. I give You my heart. I give You my life. Please heal my heart. Please lead me in my life. I want to do what You want me to do. I want to go where You want me to go. I want to say what You want me to say. I want to know freedom, God. I want to dance in fields of flowers in the light of Your Son. Amen.

Solitude

My Eden

In my garden, my place of solitude,
the gentle breeze blows through my hair,
the sun shines down on me,
the flies swarm around my neck,
and my Jesus speaks to me.

As I pull the weeds that choke the peas,
he shows me my wrong attitudes,
the spoken words,
the sinful thoughts
that choke out the fruit He tries to grow in me.
And I repent.

I see the tiny cabbage heads,
the green tomatoes,
the pea pods getting fatter,
the sunflowers reaching for new heights,
and I know what Father sees growing in me:
charity, joy, peace, patience, kindness, goodness,
faithfulness, gentleness, self-control,
a willingness to attain His character.

Here I sweat, I toil, I ache.

Here I listen, I ponder, I change…

In my Eden.

Awake, O North wind and come, wind of the South, make my garden breathe out fragrance, let its spices be wafted abroad.

Song of Solomon, 4:16
(New American Standard Bible)

A garden is a lovely place, full of seeds producing fruit. A garden is full of fragrance. It's a place of peace. It's a place to rest. Your soul is like a garden. You need God to bring the wind and the rain to your soul and produce fragrant fruit in your life. But you need to take the time to rest in Him. Slow down. Enjoy some time in your Eden.

Father,
Help me to slow down so that I can hear Your voice. Help me to be completely still in Your presence. Would You produce the most lovely garden in me? Make it lovely for You. Amen.

By The River

Here by the river things move harmoniously.
The water continually flows onward
never ceasing its gurgling sound.
The leaves rustle in the whispering breeze.
The sunshine reflects off the water causing
golden flames to dance on a log protruding from the bank.
Butterflies flutter to and fro.
Bees buzz by;
now and then they stop to rest on the flowering weeds.
Dragonflies play their game of tag
in the shade of the overhanging trees.
Up above me the fluffy white cotton balls float silently by.
The peacefulness of the world around me
quiets my spirit and fills me with serenity
which can only be found in such a beautiful place...
By the river.

Behold, I am doing a new thing; now it springs forth, do you not perceive it? I will make a way in the wilderness and rivers in the desert.

Isaiah 43:19
(Revised Standard Version)

Sometimes our lives are so dry, like a desert. God tells us He will make a river in our dry places. This will be a place of relaxation, a place where we can sit and listen quietly to the bubbling flow of the river, watch the birds, butterflies, and insects as they fly around, the sky is so lovely, and the grass is green. It is in this quiet place that we hear the voice of God.

Father,
Take me to that quiet place of rest. I long to be with You. I long for You to fill me up. I'm so dry, so weary. Refresh me with Your Word. I need to hear Your voice. Show me something new, God. Amen.

PEACE

complete contentedness
a forest, vast and green
the fresh fragrance of spring flowers
a harp softly strumming
tranquility caught in one moment of time, remembered eternally
a dove descending from heaven

Peace I leave with you; my peace I give you. I do not give to you as the world gives. Do not let your hearts be troubled and do not be afraid.

John 14:27
(New International Version)

Peace is defined as tranquility or serenity, stillness and silence. If you think of that in terms of this world, you would imagine a field of flowers or imagine you are sitting by a bubbling brook or on a sandy lake shore. God's peace is different. You can be sitting in your car in a traffic jam knowing you will be late for work, and you can feel God's peace. You can be sitting in a stressful business meeting and feel His peace. God's peace is something inside you that gives you assurance and rest even in the middle of strife. Its sweet. But you can only have it if you know Him. Think of someone who doesn't know that kind of peace and reach out to him or her today.

Father,
I need to know Your peace. I need to know Your rest. My days get so busy and hectic and stressful. It's nice to know Your peace in the middle of it all. It is so sweet. Show me someone today who doesn't know Your peace. Give me boldness to show them who You are. Amen.

communion
refining, rewarding
yet convicting, breaking, humbling
it is sharing the Sacrament in silence
refilled, refreshed, revealed
it is forgiveness and healing
intimate fellowship

And He took bread, gave thanks and broke it, and gave it to them, saying, "This is my body given for you; do this in remembrance of me."

Luke 22:19
(New International Version)

In the same way, after the supper He took the cup, saying, "This cup is the new covenant in my blood, which is poured out for you."

Luke 22:20
(New International Version)

Noah Webster says communion is "an intimate relationship with deep understanding." We experience this when we eat the bread and drink from the cup at the "communion table". But wouldn't you like to experience this every day? In fact, every moment of every day? This is what God wants for us, and this goal is attainable. This is why the Bible says to "pray without ceasing". (I Thessalonians 5:17) When we have constant communion with Him we come a little closer to "perfecting holiness in the fear of God". (II Corinthians 7:1)

Father,
I desire to have constant communion with You. I don't want the cares of this world to keep me from You. I don't want to get so busy that I don't think of You every moment. God, You walk beside me every day. I need You. Amen.

The Good Portion

Once I was like Martha,
so busy receiving, serving, ministering,
yet crying out for time alone with Jesus.
And Jesus told me,
"Be like Mary.
Stop running;
sit at my feet and listen
to what I am saying to you.
Hear me now,
and the Word you hear
will never leave you

Martha had a sister called Mary, who sat at the Lord's feet listening to what He said. But Martha was distracted by all the preparations that had to be made.

Luke 10:39-40a
(New International Version)

It's so easy to get caught up in the busy-ness of life. It's so easy to get distracted. All the while, Jesus is calling us to come into His presence and to listen to His voice. He wants us to listen to Him. If we have the radio or TV on, we might miss something. If our attention is on the things of this world, we might not hear His voice. It's vital to take time to be quiet before Him.

Father,
I'm going to be quiet now. Speak to me. I'm listening. I want the good portion. Amen.

I come to the garden alone;
I come to the center of quiet;
I come to fulfill my call;
I come to meet with you, Jesus.

I listen in the garden alone;
I listen in the center of quiet;
I listen to fulfill my call;
I listen to You, Jesus.

I go from the garden with Jesus;
I go from the center of quiet;
I go to fulfill my call;
I go with You, Lord Jesus.

I heard Thy voice in the garden…

Genesis 3:10
(King James Version)

Adam, the first man to live on this earth heard God's voice in the garden. God visited Adam in the quiet and stillness of the garden. Do we even know what it means to be still? To be quiet? Where is your garden? Find your quiet place and listen to God's voice. God was all that Adam had, so it must have been easy for him. It's not so easy now. But we must find our quiet place.

Father,
I'm in my garden now. It's so quiet here. There is stillness. And here You are. I'm listening… speak to me…Amen.

The Trinity

God
omnipotent, omnipresent
fearsome, mystifying, miraculous
the Alpha and the Omega
creative, emotional, imaginative
loving, kind
Daddy

"Abba, Father…"
Mark 14:36

Even Jesus cried, referring to God, the Creator, the Almighty One as "Abba, Father". At the time of His deepest need, Jesus cried out, "Abba, Father!" In one breath Jesus asked His Father, His Daddy, to "remove this cup from me", and in the next breath Jesus says, "Yet not my will, but what you will." Jesus needed His Daddy to listen to His heart. Jesus was alone and talking to His Daddy. Oh, how we need to get alone to be with our Abba.

Father,
You are the most wonderful Daddy anybody could ever have, and You're mine. What a precious thought. Amen.

He is:
    God, Abba…
        omnipotent, yet Daddy.

    Jesus, Savior…
        gentle, yet crucified…
            and risen!

    Spirit, Counselor…
        ever present within us,
            and our Guiding Light.

He is:
    the Trinity…
        forever and ever.

Therefore, go and make disciples of all the nations, baptizing them in the name of the Father and the Son and the Holy Spirit. Teach these new disciples to obey all the commands I have given you. And be sure of this: I am with you always, even to the end of the age.

Matthew 28:19-20
(New Living Translation)

Although the word "trinity" is not found in the Bible, it stems from the belief that our God is a "triune" God, a God with three persons, and Matthew 28:19 is one of the few places where the three persons are mentioned all together. Our God has no beginning and no end. This is unfathomable. Our God is our Father, our Savior, and our Counselor. We see him as our Father when we need comfort, our Savior when we come to an understanding of what hell is, and our Counselor when we need wisdom and insight. What an amazing God we serve!

Father, Jesus, Holy Spirit,
You are an amazing God that You can be so much to me. You come to me in my need, whatever it is: Comforter, Savior, Counselor. I need You to be all these things to me. I thank You for who You are. Amen.

The Only One

I'm the One who is always here for you.
When all of your other friends have left you in the dark,
I'll be your light.
When you're pressured by work and extracurricular activities,
talk to me;
I'll give you strength.
When you're angry, call my name:
I'll calm your spirit and give you peace.
When you're all alone, talk to me,
and I'll share with you.
When you need someone to cry to, my shoulder is always dry.
It's me,
your Comforter.
I'm the One who will tell you
that you're important and even precious
when others laugh at you because of your mistake.
It's me, your constant friend.
I'm the only One who can make you so happy deep inside
that even when things go wrong,
you will still be able to sing and smile.
It's me, the Lord.
I'm the only One who can see everything you hide from others
and all that is wrong in your life and still say,
"I love you, and I forgive you."
And I'm the only One to whom every knee shall bow
and every tongue confess…
because I am the Lord.
I am Jesus.

Jesus told him, "I am the way, the truth, and the life. No one can come to the Father except through me."

John 14:6
(New Living Translation)

In other words, Jesus is everything we will ever need! He is the Light in our darkest night, showing us the way. He is Truth when we hear all the lies from the enemy of our souls. And He is Life when all around us is darkness and death.

Father,
You are everything that I will ever need. You fill the deep and empty space inside of me. You are my Father, and You provide what I need. You meet me where I am. You're my best friend. Amen.

Heaven's Hound Dog

He knows each field you cross;
He can run just as fast.
He knows each mountain you climb;
He can climb higher, and pass!
He knows every river and lake you swim;
He can swim and never drown.
He knows every tree you climb;
He'll bark til you come down.

You can't get away from God's Spirit;
He knows every hiding place.
He knows what you say and think and feel
and he sees when you fall in the race.
He'll help you to stand firm
and give you what you want;
You'll never want Him to leave –
He's such a wonderful confidante.

Do you not know that you are the temple of God and that the Spirit of God dwells in you?

I Corinthians 3:16
(New American Standard Bible)

If God Himself lives in you, how can you possibly hide from Him? Where could you possibly go to get away from Him? He's everywhere! And if you are his child, He dwells inside of you. He gives you breath; He gives you life. Why would you want to hide from Him? You can't hide your sin from Him either. You don't have any secret that God doesn't already know. Nothing is hidden from Him.

Father,
You know me so well – better than anybody, because You created me. I know I can't hide from You, and I can't hide anything from You. Thank You, God, for making me as I am. And thank You for dwelling in me. Amen.

A Carpenter

Why did the Father choose carpentry as the occupation of our Savior?

He could've made Jesus to be a jeweler;
then He would've been in touch with the riches of the world.
But all the riches belong to Him anyway.

He could've made Jesus to be a musician;
then He could join with all the angels to worship the Father.
But that would have made Him less than what He is.

He could've made Jesus to be a fisherman;
he probably would have caught more fish than anyone.
Then where would be the lesson in fishing for men?

He could've made Jesus to be a potter;
then people would have seen Him creating beautiful things.
But what is more beautiful than creation itself?

No, the Father made Jesus to be a carpenter.
In being a carpenter
Jesus could mend broken hearts
and rebuild ruined lives.

"The thief's purpose is to steal and kill and destroy. My purpose is to give them a rich and satisfying life."

John 10:10
(New Living Translation)

The whole purpose of Jesus' coming to earth, of course, is to provide us a way to God and ultimately, to heaven. But while we are on this earth, don't you think, then, that Father would want us to live a happy, fruitful, abundant, and productive life?

Father,
Thank You for sending Jesus to this earth as a carpenter. He has rebuilt my life, and He has mended my broken heart. He has given me abundant life. Thank You, God! Amen.

The Key

Father, You hold the key to this bondage.
Your Son, Jesus, was in hell three days
so that He could steal this key from Satan,
and I could be free.

Jesus, please use the key to unlock the door, and set me free.
Give me the strength to walk through the door into freedom.

Spirit, give me wisdom on this freedom journey
to follow Father's lead, to go where He wants me to go,
and do what He wants me to do.

It was for freedom that Christ set us free; therefore, keep standing firm and do not be subject again to a yoke of slavery.

Galatians 5:1
(New American Standard Bible)

Those who do not know Jesus are slaves to sin. God wants us, as His children, to be free from sin. Unfortunately, we choose to sin sometimes. It's when we do it habitually that we once again become slaves to it. Why would we, as children of the Most High God, choose to sin and do it habitually? I would have to say that it's because we are not living as close to Christ as we should. We aren't spending time in His presence as we should. We don't pray enough, and we don't read the Bible enough. Perhaps we're feeling guilty, so we don't go to church regularly. The closer we live to Christ, the less we want to sin.

Father,
I don't want to sin anymore. I don't want to be a slave to sin. I want to live close to Your heart, God. Help me to be disciplined and obedient to You. Amen.

Father,
for You I am a clay pot that has been broken,
so that You can remake me –
an open vessel for Your use.

Jesus,
for You I am a candle,
and Your precious love has melted my heart.

Holy Spirit,
for you I am a child –
       dependent,
       watching,
       waiting,
for You to lead me in the right direction.

Father,
recreate me.

Jesus,
make me humble.

Holy Spirit,
cause me to be obedient.

…I have become like a broken vessel.

Psalm 31:12
(Revised Standard Version)

Hear, my son, and be wise, and direct your mind in the way.

Proverbs 23:19
(Revised Standard Version)

If we are broken, then there is plenty of opportunity for Christ to remake us. If our hearts are yielded to Christ, then our hearts will be melted. And if we are wise, then we will follow Christ. We need the Holy Spirit to guide us, to give us that gentle nudge.

Father,
Melt my heart for You. Lead me. Guide me in Your path. I want to follow Your lead. Just show me where You want me to go. I will go for You. Amen.

God

Daddy,
you are my Daddy.
It's You I call upon when I cry.
If I hurt inside,
and I'm all alone,
I crawl upon Your lap,
You wipe away my tears
as I cuddle up to You.
You wrap Your arms of love around me,
hug me,
kiss my forehead,
hold me…
You're my Daddy.

So you have not received a spirit that makes you fearful slaves. Instead, you received God's Spirit when He adopted you as His own children. Now we call Him "Abba, Father."

Romans 8:15
(New Living Translation)

The God who created the universe is our Father. God is our Daddy! My fondest and earliest memory is of my father and me. When I was about 3 years old, one cold winter afternoon my dad was sitting in his favorite chair. I climbed up onto my dad's lap to snuggle into his warm chest. He was wearing my favorite sweater. It was a soft warm tan sweater that buttoned down the front. I remember feeling so warm and safe as I cuddled up to my dad. I truly believe that my Father in heaven gave me this memory of my dad and me so that it would be easy for me to relate to my Father in heaven this way. It's easy to call Him Abba, Daddy.

Father,
Abba, Daddy. Those are such rich words. How good it is to climb upon Your lap and snuggle with You. It's so safe and comfortable! Thank You for being Abba to me. Amen.

Testimony

Testimony

After hurting, Lord,
You are so faithful to provide for me
a warm blanket of healing.

After the comforting, Lord,
You are so wise to give me
compassion for others who hurt.

After the mercy, Lord,
You are good to grant me boldness
to tell others about You.

Shine through me, Lord,
with comfort, compassion, and courage.

Share each other's burdens, and in this way obey the law of Christ.

Galatians 6:2
(New Living Translation)

After you've gone through something traumatic, and you see how the Lord played a part in the situation, you have a testimony to share. But more than that, God can use you to be a support to someone else who is going down the same path. God wants us to help others to get through the hard times. He wants us to encourage others.

Father,
I know that every time You take me through a dark place, it is a success story that can be used for Your glory. Bring someone into my path who is going through that same dark place, and make me sensitive to know that You ordained this meeting. Then make me bold enough to stand with this person and help her through it. Amen.

Made For You

I was made to love You,
    to worship You,
      to bless Your holy name.

I was made to live for You,
    to surrender to You,
      to pursue You.

I was made to be in Your presence,
    to breathe in Your lovely fragrance,
      to make You smile.

I was made to be touched by You,
    to feel Your fire burn in me.
      to have Your anointing on my life.

I was made to be pure for You.
    to be innocent,
      to be real.
I was made to be a vessel
to share Your love with others,
because others need to know Your forgiveness.

I was made for You.

"But be very careful to obey all the commands and the instructions that Moses gave to you. Love the Lord your God, walk in all His ways, obey His commands, hold firmly to Him, and serve Him with all your heart and all your soul."

Joshua 22:5
(New Living Translation)

Joshua was speaking to the tribes of Reuben, Gad, and the half-tribe of Manasseh after they had helped to conquer the land on the west side of the Jordan River. They were now ready to settle down in their own land. He was instructing them to obey God so that they would be blessed as a nation. The principle is very simple: We are created to obey God, obey His laws, and serve Him. This is why we are here. And in doing this we will inevitably serve others and show them the love of God. The goal, then, is to bring them to Christ. Yes, it's really quite simple.

Father,
If this is so simple why do I make it so difficult? Oh, yes, because I get in the way. God, help me to stay out of the way so that You can accomplish what You want to through me. Amen.

Come Back

I failed you, Lord.
I wandered away.
I got too busy
and I started to stray.

The cares of this life,
the busy-ness of my day
just sort of took over –
they took me away.

I didn't even realize –
it happened so fast!
Then something jogged my memory;
something from my past.

I remembered the moments
that I spent with You.
Time immersed in Your Word
made me feel fresh and new.

I'm hungry again,
and I'm so thirsty, too.
I need Your Spirit
to fill me anew!

Awaken my heart, Lord,
fill me up; satisfy me.
It's You that I want;
You are all that I need.

But the cares of the world, and the delight in riches, and the desire for other things, enter in and choke the word, and it proves unfruitful.

Mark 4:19
(Revised Standard Version)

All it takes is one bad movie or TV show to draw you away. All it takes is working too much or too hard. Just one day without God's Word will pull you away from Him. The enemy (Satan) will use anything (or anyone) to keep you from getting close to God. But when you fall or stray, God is always right there waiting for you to return. He is so faithful!

Father,
Thank You for always being there to draw me back to You. Thank You for Your Word and Your promises. Awaken my heart, oh God, and satisfy me. Amen.

Faith is…

something we always want more of,

knowing you'll always make it,

believing in something you cannot see,

powerful – even when it is as small as a mustard seed…

We do this by keeping our eyes on Jesus, the champion who initiates and perfects our faith.

Hebrews 12:2
(New Living Translation)

In chapter 11 of Hebrews, 17 of the verses begin with the words "by faith" and go on to give an example of a person in the Bible who had faith for something in his or her life. So first we begin to know Jesus, then our faith grows, and Jesus makes it perfect. He is always the finisher! He completes everything! He is the beginning and the end. Christians can't live without faith. And faith is something that you can't have too much of.

Father,
Help my faith to grow. I want to believe more, trust more, know more. Enlighten my understanding, Father. Amen.

Trade In

Like the old and rusted lamp with the useless wires
that just takes up space in the corner of the living room,
so also some junk just takes up space in my heart.
Garbage…like
     selfishness,
          jealousy,
               anger…

Just as we throw that old lamp away and replace it with a new one,
I also throw away my old self, daily;
I replace it with new and better things…like
     self-denial,
          harmony,
               joy.

Blessed are the pure in heart, for they shall see God.

Matthew 5:8
(New American Standard Bible)

Who doesn't want to see God! And who wants to keep junk? Who likes new things better than old things? God can make us new every day just like His mercies are new every morning. Yes, new is good.

Father,
I want to live in self-denial. I want peace and joy in my life. I know that You give peace, so please give me Your peace. Help me to give up selfishness, jealousy, and anger. Give me newness every day, I ask in Jesus name. Amen.

Clouded Vision

I saw the weeds
and not the peas, green beans, and carrots.

I saw the dark, ominous clouds
instead of the rainbow.

I saw the deep dark forest
instead of the wide open field.

I saw the snow covering the fresh green grass
but not the purple crocus poking through the snow.

I felt the cold north wind today
forgetting that yesterday I wore shorts.

As a result, I saw something different,
something new I thought I should have.
I took my eyes off my goal, my dream.
I began to dream a new dream – thinking it was from God.
I wondered if He had changed His mind
or if I had been walking down the wrong road all this time.
I continually ran to Him for answers,
daily calling out to Him.
I cried rivers of tears
feeling discontented, alone, weary, quiet, unsettled, wondering,
        wandering…

Then I was reminded of the basics.
I asked for strength to accept those things I cannot change,
courage to change the things I could change,
and the wisdom to know the difference between the two.
Then I was able to take joy in the middle of uncomfortable circumstances
because I was Christ in the center of it all.
Then my vision was clear.

Open Thou mine eyes, that I may behold wondrous things out of Thy law.

Psalm 119:18
(King James Version)

Why is it so easy sometimes to see the negative instead of the positive, to see the glass as half empty rather than half full? Sometimes all we need is to change our perspective. It can be done. If we really want it bad enough, Christ can and will make our vision clear so that we can see what He wants us to see…so that we see things the way He wants us to see them…the positive instead of the negative.

Father,
Help me to see things in the positive – help me to see things from Your vantage point. What do you see, God? There is nothing "negative" in You. Oh, God, I want to see what You see. Amen.

More Of You

Stretch out my heart, Oh, God.
Pull on every side to make that part of me as big as You:

longer than the longest river,
wider than the heavens,
higher than the mountains,
deeper than the sea.

Then You can fill my heart with:
       more agape love,
       more compassion,
       more empathy,
       more sympathy,
       more mercy…
       than I've ever had before.

Lord, if You will fill my heart with more of You,
then I'll be able to give to others:
       more of me…
       more of You…

Blessed are the poor in spirit…those who mourn…the gentle…those who hunger and thirst for righteousness…the merciful…the pure in heart…the peacemakers…

Matthew 5:3-9

Oh, to have more of God! More of His love and compassion…more mercy…more understanding. The more we have of God, the more we can give to those who don't know Him. Think about what it was like before you knew God. Now think of those around you who are without Him. It's our destiny to tell them about Christ.

Father,
I want to have more of You so that I can give You to the world! I want to have Your heart. I want to know Your heartbeat. I want to know what moves You. Show me today someone who doesn't know You, and make me bold enough to share You with that person. Amen.

Revelation I

Let it go, my child (He says).
Can't you see you're in bondage?
The only way you can be set free
is if you give me all of that garbage.

When you gave yourself to me,
wasn't it ALL of you?
Not just bits and pieces now and then,
every day you can be made new

Now, my Holy Spirit will come around
and tell you what to change in your life.
Please, don't rebel; obey me instead.
It will save you a lot of strife.

If you're disobedient in even one thing,
then you'll do it again and again.
Pretty soon it will be too easy
to turn away and never listen.

I love you more than you can know;
you are my own precious child.
If you desire to please me,
you will grow to be meek and mild.

The fruit of my Holy Spirit will grow in you
and people will see that and know
that there is something different about you.
You share it with them, and they can change and grow.

Stand fast therefore in the liberty wherewith Christ hath made us free, and be not entangled again with the yoke of bondage.

Galatians 5:1
(King James Version)

…and be renewed in the spirit of your mind…

Ephesians 4:23
(King James Version)

But the fruit of the Spirit is love, joy, peace, longsuffering, gentleness, goodness, faith, meekness, temperance: against such things there is no law.

Galatians 5:22
(King James Version)

Oh, to be renewed daily! Oh, that the temptation to sin were not even there! Oh, if we just wouldn't disobey! If only it were so simple. Life can be so difficult at times because God wants to test our faithfulness to Him. We need to be overcomers, and it's by the power of the Holy Spirit that we do overcome. Perhaps we are tested so that we will know that we can't do things in our own strength. We need God.

Father,
I want to overcome sin. I don't want to be subject to that yoke of slavery. I want to obey You in everything. I want people to see the fruit of the Spirit in me. I want to be more patient, more kind, more gentle. I want to be found faithful to You. Amen.

Hosea and Gomer

You married her.
But she was unfaithful to you,
so she turned and left you.
Your heart must have been broken.
Yet your love for her was unconditional.

And then you saw her in filthy rags;
she was being sold as a slave.
Your wife…a slave?
Yes…
And so you bought me back.
Your love was still the same.
Though my sins were red like crimson
They were made white like snow;
and now I am being changed into Your likeness
from one degree of glory to another.

"Come now, let's settle this," says the Lord. "Though your sins are like scarlet, I will make them as white as snow. Though they are red like crimson, I will make them as white as wool…"

Isaiah 1:18
(New Living Translation)

God spoke this to Isaiah in a vision. We now show this scripture to people when they come to Christ. What an amazing verse! Some stains just don't come out of clothes, and the stain of sin seems permanent. People without Christ are wearing filthy rags compared to the white clothes that Christians wear. God the Father removes the stain of sin from us through the blood of His Son Jesus. Are we thankful for the blood shed for us?

Father,
You accepted me in my filthy rags, and You made me white as snow. Thank You for giving Your Son to shed His blood for me so that I could be clean. Amen.

Victory

Pure and white like fresh snow;
that's what I want you to be.
Fresh and beautiful as a bouquet
with a lovely fragrance; that's me.

I want to suffer like Jesus
and really know what He felt.
I want to feel the same heartbreak;
I want my pride to melt.

I know I am a conqueror in this world of sinful men.
This spiritual battle is hard,
but I have victory in the end,
because this is the victory that God has promised me:
I can do all things through Christ
who strengthens me.

For I can do everything through Christ, who gives me strength.

Philippians 4:13
(New Living Translation)

If we try to do things in our own strength, we may fail. But if we allow Christ to be the strength in us, we never fail if what we do is according to His will.

Father,
Be victorious in me. I can win every battle with you by my side. Be strong in me. Take away my pride so that I can give You the glory. Amen.

I'm So Glad!

I'm glad I'm alive; I'm glad I'm free;
I'm happy that Jesus is living in me.

I heard Him one day when He called my name.
He beaconed; He promised; and I gladly came.

He told me what He had done for me -
how He had died on the cross at Gethsemane.

I gave Him my life, I gave Him my all.
I gave Him my promise to follow His call.

I walk in His footsteps; He helps me each day.
He gives me the strength to follow His way.

One day soon (I'm sure it will be!)
He'll come back to this earth for me.

He'll take me home to heaven above
where I will live in His kindness and love.

I'm so glad I'm alive – I'm so glad I am free!
I'm so happy that Jesus is living in me!

Restore to me the joy of Your salvation, and make me willing to obey You.

Psalm 51:12
(New Living Translation)

Do you ever take for granted the fact that you are going to heaven? Isn't it a relief to know you have escaped the fire of hell? Shouldn't you tell the whole world about this? Our relationship with God is so personal, and yet it needs to be shared. Do you have a family member or good friend who does not know Jesus? Pray right now that this important person will come to know Jesus.

Father,
It's so good to know that I will live eternally with You in heaven! I am Your bride, ready, waiting for You to come and take me away. But, God, I have friends and family members who do not yet know You. I pray, God, that You would reveal Yourself to them and they would surrender to You. Amen.

Rejoice!

Does Jesus care?
     He's always there.
          He wipes your tears,
              takes away your fears.
     Jesus is always there.

Jesus loves!
     He will forgive.
          He erases your guilt,
              heals your hurt.
     Jesus will always forgive.

Jesus lives!
     He will come back.
          The story's been told;
              the world He holds!
     Jesus is coming back!

So praise His name!
     Rejoice in the Lord!
          Shine your light
              in the darkest night,
And always rejoice in the Lord.

"I will never desert you, nor will I ever forsake you."

Hebrews 13:5
(New American Standard Bible)

"…your iniquity is taken away, and your sin is forgiven."

Isaiah 6:7
(New American Standard Bible)

…and that He was buried, and that He was raised on the third day according to the scriptures."

I Corinthians 15:4
(New American Standard Bible)

It is good to give thanks to the Lord and to sing praises to Your name, O Most High.

Psalm 92:1
(New American Standard Bible)

Do you feel guilty? Or perhaps lonely? You're a Christian, and yet you feel these things because God gave us humans these feelings. You know that He is alive, so take comfort in knowing that Jesus is with you, and He has forgiven you. So rejoice in Him and take joy in His salvation.

Father,
When I am at my lowest point, help me to remember who You are and that You are with me. Help me to take the negative feelings and thoughts and replace them with praise for You. Thank You, Jesus, that You are alive! Amen.

The Nature of Things

God's Beauty

As I sit by the water on the shore of Lake Michigan
I notice the nature around me...
>how miraculous it is!

I feel the grains of sand as they sit in the palm of my hand...
>how minute they are!

I see the water as it stretches out over the horizon...
the tiny diamonds of light in the distant land...
>how pretty it is!

I see the seagulls flying through the sky
and floating on the water – calling...
>how free they are!

I see the sky all pink and red;
the sun a big bright orange ball sinking into the water...
>how beautiful it is!

I feel the love of God in the beauty of nature all around me...
>how great He is!

For the Lord is great, and greatly to be praised: He is to be feared above all gods.

Psalm 96:4
(King James Version)

Can you imagine what the days of creation must have been like? I think God was having fun! I like to think that He played with the sand that He created. I like to think that He was in the water to make it just the right temperature, feeling the pokey needles of the pine tree that He made, petting the soft fur of the rabbit, listening carefully to the cooing of the mourning dove and the meowing of the cat. Can you imagine Him painting the sky that first evening after He had made the day? God is so amazing…

Father,
You amaze me. Thank You for giving me the things of this world to enjoy. You are worthy of praise, God, for all that You made. You are so good. Amen.

A Promise

The sky is dull gray, threatening...
and the wind howls through the naked trees
breaking the brittle branches;
But the trees do not need to protect themselves;
they are sound asleep, lost to the world.
The ground is frozen, hard and brown...
waiting...just waiting...
to be buried beneath sparkling drifts of snow,
vowed to be formed with loving hands.
Then...
the first snowflake, daring and valiant,
slowly and cautiously drifts downward
from its heavenly home.
It is followed by a parade of other snowflakes,
all doomed to be lost in a howling wind...
yet used to create something beautiful.

Lead me in Your truth and teach me, for You are the God who saves. All day long I put my hope in You.

Psalm 25:5
(New Living Translation)

We must wait for God like we wait for the winter snow. Sometimes the snow comes quickly, and sometimes God does, too. Waiting forces us to develop patience, one of the fruits of the Spirit. We have to remember that God's timing is perfect; ours is not. Shouldn't we trust Him more than we trust ourselves and others?

Father,
Help me to be patient as I wait for things. I don't want to rush anything. Help me to remember that Your timing is perfect. You have everything under Your control. I trust You, God. Amen.

Omnipresence

You are always with me;
    I am aware of Your presence.

I can't see You in person,
Yet I see You in:
    soaring mountains
    streaking lightning
    fleeting butterflies…

I don't hear Your voice,
but You whisper all around me in:
    the whipping wind
    birds love songs
    resounding raindrops…

I smell Your newness in:
    pinecones
    fresh strawberries
    dandelions and daisies…

Your freshness is tasted in:
    green grapes
    sweet canes of sugar
    picked peas…

I feel Your gentleness in:
    a baby's soft smooth skin
    carpets of green grass
    warmth of sunshine…

Yes, You are with me always.
Your presence is awesome.

For He has said, "I will never fail you nor forsake you." Hence we can confidently say, "The Lord is my helper, I will not be afraid; what can man do to me?"

Hebrews 13:5-6
(Revised Standard Version)

The author of Hebrews was referring to Deuteronomy 31:6 where Moses tells the Israelites that God will not abandon them as they go into the Promised Land. God was with them in the fire by night and the cloud by day, and He would stay with them and lead them. Now it is different. We experience God's presence in a whole new way because we have the Holy Spirit. He lives in us!

Father,
When I'm lonely, You are right by my side. When I'm sad, You're right there to dry my tears. When I'm angry, You are with me to calm me. When I'm afraid, You hold my hand. And when I'm feeling fine, You are walking beside me. Thank You for never leaving me. Amen.

Changes

Just as the snow melts and flowers bloom in spring,
so renewal comes and sin is purged when the Spirit comes alive.

As tears are refreshment for damaged emotions,
so the Spirit quenches a thirsty soul and heals a hurting heart.

As a cloud lingers and then turns to moisture and waters the earth,
so the Spirit of God hovers, waiting for people to receive Him.

As a butterfly softly and quietly alights upon goldenrod,
so the Holy Spirit gently comes upon us.

As the earth brings forth shoots,
and as a garden causes what is sown in it to spring up,
so the Lord will cause righteousness and praise
to spring forth before all nations.

As the deer pants for water,
so longs my soul after Thee, O Lord.

And as a lamp lights the darkness and overcomes it,
so does Jesus in me shine forth and make me victorious.

And it will come about after this that I will pour out My Spirit on all mankind, and your sons and your daughters will prophesy, your old men will dream dreams, your young men will see visions.

Joel 2:28
(New American Standard Bible)

The Spirit of God:
  Causes people to prophesy (I Sam. 10:10)
  Searches (I Cor. 2:10)
  Discerns spiritual things (I Cor. 2:14)
  Lives in His people (I Cor. 3:16)
  Justifies and sanctifies (I Cor. 6:11)
  Guides us (John 16:13)

Father,
Thank You for Your Holy Spirit that lives in me. I want to prophesy! I want Your Spirit to search my heart. I want to be able to discern spiritual things by the power of Your Spirit. I need Your Spirit to guide my way. God, pour out Your Spirit on me. Amen.

One Sunday Morning

I watched a squirrel today.
He picked up a walnut, placed it in his mouth,
and clung to it as he climbed up a tree to his favorite limb.
There he sat, and he picked at the walnut,
peeling off the outer green shell.
Then I watched as the walnut fell from his paws.
The squirrel looked to see where his food had fallen,
climbed down the tree trunk,
retrieved his treasure,
and climbed back up the tree to his favorite spot,
and he played with it some more.

Now I think,
how like that squirrel I am.
How often do I take hold of something,
good or bad,
and tear at it, play with it, and finally drop it
at Jesus' feet...
only to retrieve it and tear at it, play with it,
and hold onto it longer?

But then I watched the squirrel climb back down the tree,
find his favorite spot in the yard,
and bury his walnut there.

Maybe I can learn to bury everything that is mine
at Jesus' feet so that He can have it all,
and I will never take it back again.

My father taught me, "Take my words to heart. Follow my commands, and you will live. Get wisdom; develop good judgment…take hold of my instructions; don't let them go. Guard them, for they are the key to life."

Proverbs 4:4,13
(New Living Translation)

Some things, like God's Word, His commandments, wisdom, and understanding (instruction), we need to hold fast to. We need to look for them, acquire them, and hold on to them. If we do, our life will be better, perhaps even easier. Certainly, if we have wisdom, we might make fewer mistakes, thus avoiding trouble in this life. Squirrels will bury their treasure and find it at a later date. They store up for a time of need. That's wise.

Father,
I want wisdom and understanding. I want to know and follow Your commandments and Your Word. Give me a hunger to seek Your face. Let me not be satisfied with little. Amen.

Pussywillow Christians

I am the first bud in spring,
pure and white,
precious and soft,
shining and bright,
just like my Creator.
I am beautiful because He made me.
My brothers and sisters shine as I do –
we are the only brightness
in the dull, drab surroundings.
But soon, I know, because of the intensity
of the life within us,
others will be filled with new Life;
They, too, will be set free.
After all, my Creator is their Creator,
and He makes all things beautiful.

For it is written, "As I live, says the Lord, every knee shall bow to me, and every tongue shall give praise to God."

Romans 14:11
(New American Standard Bible)

As some point in time every person ever created will know who God is, and they will acknowledge Him as God, the Creator and Lord of all. Some may be in hell doing so because they didn't confess Him as Lord while they lived on this earth. But for the bride of Christ, His Church, it will be a glorious time. We will be pure and white, filled with Life, and we will give praise to Him in a way that we can only touch the surface here on this earth.

Father,
When will You send Your Son to come for His bride? I long for that day. Come quickly, Lord. Amen.

Outside
The snow falls ever so softly upon the earth;
the streetlights make the snowflakes glisten like the stars in the heavens,
and the silence is deafening.
I stick out my tongue to catch a tasty flake of snow.

Just as the snow falls from heaven,
so does the Spirit of God descend.
It falls ever so gently in the midst of one hundred people - -
just as a butterfly alights upon a daisy,
and the silence draws me to Him.

Immediately coming up out of the water, He saw the heavens opening, and the Spirit like a dove descending upon Him.

Mark 1:10
(New American Standard Bible)

Can you just imagine what that must have been like? It had to be a quiet time of stillness. If anyone was watching, they must have caught their breath. I'll bet you could have missed it if you had blinked. I've heard people say that the Spirit of God is a gentleman. He doesn't force His way into anything or any place. He has to be invited in. Jesus was ready to begin His earthly ministry, and He needed God's Spirit to lead Him. We need to follow His example, be baptized, and ask the Spirit to lead us. We need the guidance of the Holy Spirit. We need the Holy Spirit to draw us to Him.

Father,
Thank You for Your gentle Holy Spirit. Draw me to You, Father, so that we can run together. I need the quiet and the stillness so that I can hear Your voice. Amen.

miracle…
budding maple leaf,
golden fields of wheat,
blooming tulip,
double rainbow,
clouds like cotton,
thundering ocean,
swift flowing river,
graceful swan,
newborn baby,
a friend heaven sent…
you

A friend loveth at all times…

Proverbs 17:17
(King James Version)

Let's face it; we need each other. Everyone needs a friend. No one wants to go through this life completely alone. Jesus had 12 close friends. A good friend is like a miracle and a gift from God. He knows we need friends, so He sends certain people into our lives. He will also remove people from our lives that He knows we do not need. Our Father knows what is best for us.

Father,
Thank You for my friends. I need friends, but I want You to be my best friend. I want You to be the one that I talk to most, the one that I depend on most. And please send into my life the people that I need as friends. Give me a new friend and make me a friend to someone. Amen.

Everything

I see You –
    in snow-capped mountains,
    in the smiling face of a child,
    in fields of wheat,
    in the single cloud in the clear blue sky

I hear You –
    in the wind rustling through the trees,
    in the ocean waves crashing on the shore,
    in the sweet sound of a harp,
    in the birds' songs

I feel You –
    in the softness of a baby's skin,
    in the sand between my toes,
    in the cushion of grass beneath my feet,
    in the hug of a friend.

You are the fragrance of a lilac bush,
You are the air that I breathe,
You are the melody if my heart,
You are the path through the dark, dense forest – the way out.

You are everything to me,
and everything that I need.

Blessed are those who hunger and thirst for righteousness, for they shall be satisfied.

Matthew 5:6
(New American Standard Bible)

Why would we want to look for satisfaction in a book, a bottle, a weed, a person, or a picture? Jesus is everything we need. He satisfies our hungry hearts, our thirsty souls. He is everything, and He is in everything. Why would we want to look for something else?

Father,
Help me to not look aside from You. I don't want to be distracted by the things of this world. You created this world for me to enjoy, but You never intended that anything in this world would satisfy my soul. Only You can do that. You are my everything. I love You, Father. Amen.

History

Time

Time goes by so quickly, Lord;
each tomorrow is all too quickly becoming

> a bittersweet memory,
> a horrifying recollection,
> a joyful experience…

even before I have a chance to anticipate it.
Too much is going on in each today
to even think about each tomorrow.

Sure,
I know I should simply live "one day at a time"
but please…
give me time to dream.

"For I know the plans I have for you," says the Lord. "They are plans for good and not for disaster, to give you a future and a hope."

Jeremiah 29:11
(New Living Translation)

God has a plan for each one of His children. Sometimes it's in the dreams we have as children. Sometimes it's not revealed until we are adults. But God has a plan, and He will show us what it is. It must be our goal in life to seek God's face for His plan and purpose for our being here. Sometimes we may dream as children, and we don't see the plan come to fruition until much later in life. The end result is always good, and God's timing is perfect.

Father,
I want to know the plans that You have for me. I want to go where You want me to go. I want to do what You want me to do. Let me dream the dreams that You want me to dream. Amen.

The Ladder of the Lord

I was on the ground;
I hadn't begun to climb the ladder of the Lord.
And then I met this friend, Jesus,
and I found myself on the first rung.
I learned more about this friend, Jesus,
as I read and studied the Word;
I kept going higher and higher
on this ladder of the Lord.

I was so surprised when I looked down
and saw all those people on the ground
       looking…
         searching…
for what I had already found.
I wanted to be a part of them again
when I saw some of the things they were doing…
and then I started to fall.
I got closer and closer to them
until I once again looked up into the clouds above me
and realized that this was better!

I found Jesus was my true friend,
and the more I looked up to Him,
the higher I climbed on the ladder of the Lord.
As I opened myself to Jesus
God's Spirit filled me more
and I got closer and closer to Him.

I'm waiting for the day that I reach the top
Of the ladder of the Lord.
Then I'll see Jesus as He is…
The perfect Son of God…
And I'll be that perfect child of His
Who had climbed the ladder of the Lord.

Come close to God, and God will come close to you...

James 4:8
(New Living Translation)

This whole Christian walk is a growing process. If we settle and are satisfied where we are, we don't produce much fruit; we become stagnant. If we always want more of the Lord, and if we continue to desire to be closer to Him, we will produce abundant fruit for the Lord. Let's not be satisfied with just a little bit.

Father,
I want more of You. I want to know You more. I want wisdom and understanding. I desire to produce much fruit for You. I want people to see You in me. Amen.

Chapters

I'm stepping out of my life for awhile –
maybe for a long time.
I'm going away to try something new –
something totally different.

It's going to be hard for awhile –
it'll take some getting used to,
but I'm not going all alone,
though at times I'll feel alone;
      Jesus is going with me.

I'll just be myself, and I'll make new friends.

I'll enjoy myself and meet new people
in this new chapter of my life.

And there will be other chapters in my life –
some short and some so long,
but I'm living each day of each chapter in a very special way,
and I know I'll never really be alone.

"No man will be able to stand before you all the days of your life. Just as I have been with Moses, I will be with you; I will not fail you nor forsake you."

Joshua 1:5
(New American Standard Bible)

Moses had just died, and God appointed Joshua to take the Israelites across the Jordan River to the Promised Land. These are the words God spoke to Joshua as he was preparing to lead the people. I believe God speaks these very words to us today. God will never leave any one of His children. He will never forsake one of His children. We face transitions throughout our lives, but we are never alone in them.

Father,
What a comfort to know You are with me wherever I go! I am never alone. Sometimes the road I am on is difficult to walk, but You are always by my side. Thank You, God, for never leaving me. Amen.

Life is so full of good-byes and hellos;
thorns and roses;
threatening storm clouds and promises of peace in rainbows.
It has a lot of dark, fearful valleys
and high, majestic mountains;
frowns and smiles;
dark, ominous nights and brilliant sunny days.
Life is made of death and birth,
war and peace,
hate and love.
Life's not all bad, but it's not all good;
Satan is alive and strong,
but God's everlasting and omnipotent love
will always triumph.

The Lord appeared to him from afar saying, "I have loved you with an everlasting love; therefore, I have drawn you with lovingkindness.

Jeremiah 31:3
(New American Standard Bible)

God spoke these words to Jeremiah giving him hope for the restoration of Israel after Babylonian captivity. His love never ends. His love draws us to Him. And His love triumphs over evil. God's love is so strong.

Father,
It was Your love for me that sent You Son to the cross to die for me. Oh, God. Thank You for loving me with an everlasting love. Amen.

AGAPE

I saw you riding a donkey in a crowd –
people were waving palm branches shouting,
"Hosanna in in the highest!"
And "Here comes King Jesus!"
I wondered, "Why?"
And I heard you tell them, "I love you."

You broke bread for us; you said this was your body.
We all drank wine together; this, you said, was your blood.
It was an intimate time, and I needed to know why.
As you served us, you told us, "I love you."

I was with you when they came to take you away.
Judas kissed you.
I wanted to shout, "Why!"
You looked at me, and your silent eyes said, "I love you."

I was there when you were scourged, bleeding, hurting…
I cried and whispered, "Why?"
You looked at me and said, "I love you."

I watched you drag that heavy cross up the hill called Golgatha –
Your back was already blistered.
I asked you, "Why?"
You answered, "Because I love you."

They hammered the nails in your wrists and feet.
I ran – I couldn't take your pain – and I screamed, "Why?!"
As I ran I heard you say, "I love you."

Then you were hanging on the cross, dying, and before I could ask,
You looked down at me and whispered, "I love you."

After your body was in the tomb three days,
Suddenly you were gone!
I knew you had risen just like you had said,
and your words sounded in my mind:
"I love you."

But God showed His great love for us by sending Christ to die for us while we were still sinners.

Romans 5:8
(New Living Translation)

Jesus demonstrated His love to us in everything He said and in everything He did. He was always expressing love. It's all He could do. It's what He was destined to do…because He is love. It wasn't that He went around saying all the time, "I love you." It was more in His actions. Love is a verb – it's an action word.

Father,
Help me to demonstrate love more. Help me to show others Your perfect love. Help me to love others the way You do. Then people will come to You. Amen.

His Hands

My hands have held the hands of another
and have gently wiped away tears –
my own and those of others.
My hands have harshly slapped
and have joyfully clapped
and have rubbed some weary shoulders.
My hands have picked up a pencil to write
and have opened many books
and have turned countless pages.
They have held
> a feather,
>
> a stone,
>
> a bird,
>
> a leaf,
>
> a baby…

but of all the things my hands have done,
there is still one thing they will never do
because Jesus' hands did it for me.
His hands took the place of mine on the cross;
so my hands will never have nails driven through them,
they will never bleed like His,
they will never hold the weight of the world…
like His did…
but because His hands took the place of mine,
I want my hands to do all things for His glory.

Commit everything you do to the Lord, trust Him, and He will help you.

Psalm 37:5
(New Living Translation)

God is there to help us on this journey we call life. He did so much for us; can't we do something for Him? It doesn't have to be something huge. Our very lives being lived out for Him make all the difference. You might be just one small light in a very dark place, but you make that dark place brighter. Every hug you give offers hope. Every smile you give offers happiness. Every tear you wipe away offers compassion. When you rub someone's weary shoulders, you offer strength. Serve him in serving others, and you'll make a difference.

Father,
I want everything that I do to be done for You. Let my hands be Your hands. Let my feet be Your feet. Let my words be Your words. I want to serve You, Lord. Amen.

No Room

"Look at those Jesus Freaks walkin' the streets with Bibles in their hands,"
mocked the teenage boy to his girl.
"Man, I got better things to hold onto!"
His grin was painted on;
deep inside his heart fluttered as he drove on to the party.

"Not now," said the elderly man, an elder of the church to his wife.
"I can't go to the hospital to visit ole' Mr. Jones until the football game is over."

"Why?" the old man mumbled under his breath.
"It's ridiculous to stand outside supermarkets in this cold
ringing a stupid bell every Christmas. They just get in our way!"

"Not today," she thought while the last hymn was sung.
"I have to hurry home after church or the meatloaf will burn."

"No room," said the innkeeper to Joseph and Mary.

And she gave birth to her firstborn son, and she wrapped Him in cloths, and laid Him in a manger, because there was no room for them in the inn.

Luke 2:7
(New American Standard Bible)

I don't know how many people have actually rejected Jesus. They know He is the only One who can save them, but they actually turn their backs on Him. These must be very stubborn and independent people. Or else these people are deceived. In any case, they need Him. It's our responsibility as Christians to tell them the story again and again and bring as many people to Christ as we can. The time is short. Jesus is coming for His bride soon.

Father,
I know that I walk on by people every day who need You. Some are in desperate circumstances, and I don't even know it. Give me more compassion, Lord. Show me those with whom You have set a divine appointment for me to talk to. Give me the boldness to share You with them. It's Your desire that no one would perish. Amen.

Climbing The Hill

After falling back down the hill that had taken me years to climb,
I wondered, "Why me? How can this happen after so much time?"

I tried, oh, how hard I tried to stand back up and say,
"Look world! Look what I've done! I can handle things okay."

But when I was standing, I lost my balance and almost fell again.
"Oh, c'mon now!" I told myself, "You can do it; you know you can."

"But can I?" That was my question, and it penetrated deep in my heart.
"How can I? Something's missing." That something played the biggest part.

It was Jesus. He was missing. But didn't He laugh at my fall?
"No, I didn't laugh," He told me. "I didn't laugh at all."

"I only cried. You hurt me, you know. I love you so very much."
And then I felt it – so very soft; His gentle, comforting touch.

"Come to me, my child," He said. "Come; I'll give you peace.
I'll give you strength and courage, and a love that will never cease."

I climbed that hill by myself once, and now I've climbed it again.
This time I took Jesus with me, and I've found joy that will never end.

Enoch walked with God…

Genesis 5:22

Noah walked with God…

Genesis 6:9

For the Lord is my strength and song.

Isaiah 12:2

I wouldn't want to walk anywhere without God by my side. I would feel as if I were in a dark and very lonely place apart from God. With God there is light and there is joy. God is our strength, and He offers help to go where He wants us to go and to do what He calls us to do. If we try on our own, we will fail.

Father,
I've tried to go it alone, and the road is too difficult. The hill is too steep. I need Your help and Your strength. I need You, God. Would You go with me? Thank You, Father. Amen.

Trusting You

So many times I have laughed with You, talked with You, walked with You,
trusting You.

So many times I have sat in Your awesome presence…
and trusted You.

So many times I have crawled onto Your lap,
confused, not understanding my feelings…
and I trusted You.

So many times I have cried out to You, my heart hurting, broken…
and I trusted You.

So many times I've been angry with You,
yet, I trusted You.

So many times I have not understood Your ways…
but I trusted You.

I will trust You to the end.

Know therefore that the Lord your God is God, the faithful God who keeps covenant and steadfast love with those who love Him and keep His commandments, to a thousand generations.

Deuteronomy 7:9
(Revised Standard Version)

God is faithful to those who love Him. He will never leave us nor forsake us. We are never alone. He heals our broken hearts. He laughs with us. He gives us understanding. We can trust Him.

Father,
I trust You, God. I know You are with me. You've healed my broken heart. You've laughed with me. You give me wisdom every day. Thank You for being there, God. I trust You. Amen.

Moments

The moments slip through my fingers;

    soon to be gone,

    soon to be gone…

    Dear Lord,

You've given me each precious moment to do with it what I want.

Help me to live each moment for you

    by doing some small deed for someone else,

    by talking to You,

    by praising You,

    by worshiping You.

Help me to see You in each moment;

then every memory will be filled with You!

My soul shall be joyful in the Lord; it shall rejoice in His salvation.

Psalm 35:9
(King James Version)

What better thing is there to do every moment of every day than to praise the Lord! God has given us this life. Shouldn't we live it for Him? Shouldn't we give Him our time, our talents, our very hearts? Surrender to Christ brings freedom.

Father,
I surrender to You. My heart is Yours. My time is Yours. My life is Yours. Do with me what You will. I worship You in this moment. Amen.

Time

Yesterday –
the time I lived,
the moments gone –
spent in good or bad,
forgiveness and healing,
sowing and reaping,
happy or sad –
it's all just a memory.

Today –
the day I live in.
the moments He created for me –
right now –
to live full and free!

Tomorrow –
is not yet here,
decisions will have to be made.
what will be I don't even know.
if I care, I may worry.
I must plan with wisdom.

Today –
I sow what tomorrow I reap.
Right choices today
make good memories tomorrow.
Today I live for Him
so tomorrow I live free.

Do not be deceived, God is not mocked, for whatever a man sows, this he will also reap.

Galatians 6:7
(New American Standard Bible)

Sowing and reaping – it's what life is all about. If you give your time, you will always have enough time. If you give finances, you will always have enough. God blesses us when we give of ourselves. This is one of His principles. It's a kind of paradox, though, because aside from our very lives, what can we give to God that He doesn't already own? Therefore, we are only stewards of what we possess. So let's be the best stewards that we can possibly be. The result will be good memories.

Father,
My life is Yours. My time is Yours. My talents are Yours. So help me, Father, to be a good steward of what You have given me. I want to reap good things in this life that I live for You. I want to have happy memories. Amen.

Freedom Rings

Free

Soaring so high –
at last I am free!
I'm no longer in bondage –
locked up with no key.
For I have found Jesus,
and He's given to me
a reason to smile
and to be happy.
He wants me to help others
and to let them see
that He died for them, too,
at Gethsemane.
I have to tell others
what's happened to me
and let them know that
they, too, can be free!

For you have been called to freedom, my brothers and sisters. But don't use your freedom to satisfy your sinful nature.

Galatians 5:13
(New Living Translation)

Praise God! Christ has set us free! The joy of being free! When you are living in sin you think that you are so free – free to do whatever you want and get away with it because your conscience is dead. You don't realize that you are in bondage to sin until someone comes along and tells you the truth. The Truth (Jesus) will set you free. Then when you submit to Him, you are truly free. When you have done something wrong, and a policeman comes along to arrest you, you submit to him, the handcuffs go on, and you are in bondage. You are not free. But it's the opposite with Christ. When you submit to Him, you are free.

Father,
Thank You that I am not in bondage to sin. Thank You that I walk in freedom every day because of Jesus. Now let me serve someone else in this freedom so that they, too, can be free. Amen.

Surrender

Jesus,
I'm hurt.
I'm rejected –
    just like You were.

I know You know what I feel…

And, Jesus,
I don't have to tell You
about the tears that I cry;
You know, because You cried them, too.

And Jesus,
Abba was right there holding You, loving You
through all of Your pain.
Well…
Abba is holding me, too;
I'm not alone.

But, Jesus,
How did You overcome Your pain?

"I didn't.
That was the cause of my death.
But you don't have to die to overcome your pain."

Then what do I have to do?

"Just let me love through you.
My agape love overpowers any force.
I will be victorious in you if you let me."

"I have told you all this so that you may have peace in me. Here on earth you will have many trials and sorrows. But take heart, because I have overcome the world."

John 16:33
(New Living Translation)

Jesus has overcome any pain or trouble in this world. Therefore, when we experience pain and suffering we must "take heart" (take courage or be strong) and trust Him because He has already taken care of it for us. His love is more powerful than anything. Jesus has already experienced everything that we go through. There's nothing new for Him.

Father,
You know my pain. You've already experienced this same pain, so I know You understand. Thank You for understanding. Thank You that I am not alone in this. Thank You for Your love that overcomes pain and suffering. Amen.

Fine tune me, Father –
        like the musician tunes his guitar
        to be in perfect harmony,
        tune me to be in perfect harmony,
        tune me to be a beautiful instrument
        of worship to You, Lord.

When my music is in discord,
Father, cause me to stop and listen
and to allow You to rearrange me.

When my music gets all jumbled together,
cause me to stop and allow You to
smooth out the rough spots.

When my timing is off,
cause me to stop and open up Your Word
and be in fellowship with You.

When my music fades away,
Father, cause Your Spirit to rise up within me…
        to set my feet dancing,
        to make my heart rejoice,
        to make my mouth sing Your praises…

Fine tune me, Father,
perfect me for Your service.

And the priests waited on their offices: the Levites also with instruments of music of the Lord, which David the king had made to praise the Lord, because His mercy endureth forever...

II Chronicles 7:6
(King James Version)

David had the instruments made for the sole purpose of worshiping the Lord. He also had singers for the purpose of worship. The music was for God. Here and now the music we make might have errors in composition; in heaven it will be perfect. There can be no mistakes. The harmony will be perfect. Our voices will blend perfectly. Here and now, though, we need to allow God to "fine tune" us individually for His purpose. We need to allow Him to clean us up and to perfect us for His glory – just like David's instruments were made for His glory.

Father,
Fine tune me for Your service. Make the music of my life perfect for You. Let joy rise up in me! I will dance for You! I will worship You, God, with all my heart! As the priests and Levites used their instruments for Your glory, I want my life to be for Your glory. Amen.

I read about them:
    the hungry,
    the sick,
    the helpless…

I see them:
    the aged,
    the poor,
    the heathen…

I know them:
    the weak,
    the lonely,
    the discouraged…

And I read about Him:
    who feeds,
    who heals,
    who gives hope…

And I see Him:
    who gives life,
    who gives wonderful riches,
    who forgives…

And I know Him:
    whose joy is my strength,
    who fills my cup to overflowing,
    who lifts me up!

Oh, that the hungry, the sick, the helpless
would read about Him;
the aged, the poor, the heathen
would see Him;
the weak, the lonely, the discouraged
would know Him…
as I read about Him, see Him, and know Him.

Then these righteous ones will reply, "Lord, when did we ever see you hungry and feed you? Or thirsty and give you something to drink? Or a stranger and show you hospitality? Or naked and give you clothing? When did we ever see you sick or in prison and visit you?" And the King will say, "I tell you the truth, when you did it to one of the least of these my brothers and sisters, you were doing it to me!"

Matthew 35:37-40
(New Living Translation)

When we serve others, we serve Christ. When we give food to the local food pantry, we are giving to Jesus. When we give our old clothes to the resale shops, we are giving to God. When we go to a prison to encourage an inmate, we visit with God. When we check in on our elderly neighbor who is all alone, we are ministering to God. These little things are big things to God.

Father,
Help me to keep things in perspective. Help me to remember it's these little things that matter to You. These little things make a big difference. I want to serve You, Lord. Amen.

The Duster

I am like a precious bird sitting upon a shelf.
He is the Duster who comes and picks me up so gently
placing me in the palm of His hand.
With His other hand He takes His white cloth
with the blood stains and dusts me.
Each particle that falls from me
is like a burden lifted,
and soon I am set free,
and I am transparent.

In Him we have redemption through His blood, the forgiveness of our trespasses, according to the riches of His grace which He lavished on us, in all wisdom and insight.

Ephesians 1:7
(New American Standard Bible)

His grace is lavished on us. Let that sink in for a moment. His grace is lavished on us. Some say God's grace is unmerited favor. Lavish is extravagant or abundant, like a torrent of rain. God has that much grace...for me? Someone who says things she shouldn't? Someone who has made wrong choices? Someone with regrets? Grace lavished. Abundant favor poured out like a torrent of rain. Now that's love.

Father,
The only way we can know true love is through Your Son and His death on the cross. God, help me to not take Your abundant grace for granted. Your grace means my forgiveness and salvation. Thank You, Father. Amen.

Face The Truth

Something is buried deep inside
Thoughts trying hard to hide
Feelings pervade your mind
Buried too deep to find
Hidden emotions, unseen, unknown,
From seeds long ago sown
Drowning and struggling for air
Burdens too heavy to bear

Now surfacing, breathe deep
It's time to take that giant leap
From doubts and insecurity
To assurance and tranquility
Where you meet God face to face
And you find your resting place
Where the past is forgiven and forgotten
And the future is always certain
Where the grass is green
And the air is clean
Where the quiet river flows
And the gentle breeze blows
The sun shines bright
In God's glorious light
It's heaven on earth
Experiencing rebirth

I trust in God, so why should I be afraid? What can mere mortals do to me?

Psalm 56:11
(New Living Translation)

Look at the proud! They trust in themselves, and their lives are crooked. But the righteous will live by their faithfulness to God.

Habakkuk 2:4
(New Living Translation)

When faith and trust in God meet, one experiences rebirth, a newness of life that can only be known because of Jesus. This is the place where you know the peace that passes understanding. This is where you understand true forgiveness. This is where the quiet waters flow, where the gentle breeze blows, where the sun shines bright, and you can rest in lush green pastures. This only happens with God.

Father,
Thank You for green pastures and sunshine. I want to visit those lush green pastures by the quiet water often, Lord. I want to linger there in the stillness. Help me to pace myself in this life so that I can experience Your peace in troubled times and in good times. Thank You for saving me. Amen.

Liberty

You're forgiven –
    I've set you free –
    and you never even asked.
    The offense is pardoned.
    I choose to forget.

Now I am forgiven.
    I didn't plead.
    I asked a simple question;
    He gave a simple answer:
    Yes.

I fly like a bird.
The chains are broken.
I am free.

And forgive us our debts, as we also have forgiven our debtors.

Matthew 6:12
(New American Standard Bible)

Be kind to one another, tender-hearted, forgiving each other, just as God in Christ also has forgiven you.

Ephesians 4:32
(New American Standard Bible)

If you want to be forgiven, then you need to forgive. The freedom you experience when you forgive someone is incredible! You really do feel like a bird set free! When Jesus was on the cross it looked like He was done for – things really looked bleak and hopeless. But He was, in reality, sailing and soaring free like a bird because He was full of forgiveness! And He was setting us free at the same time.

Father,
Jesus always forgave. He spent His whole life on this earth setting people free. Help me to not hold on to anger toward someone, but instead to be forgiving, so that I can be free. Amen.